All Who Wander

Natalie McMahon

BookLeaf Publishing

India | USA | UK

Presentation by *BookLeaf Publishing*

Web: www.bookleafpub.com

E-mail: info@bookleafpub.com

ISBN: 9789357444347

First edition 2022

Pouring from an empty cup

Why is it so easy to be everything for everyone?

Like my cup doesn't empty

Until I try to get a taste
but I've already died of thirst

Sometimes in the dark, when it's hard to breathe

I long to be the sun.

Where did it go?

Every time you cut me down
I grow back faster
Taller
Stronger

Much like a rose

This flower is not yours

Why are you still with him?

To accept someone takes strength
To love someone takes courage
To stay with someone takes resolve

I have that much
Even if he doesn't

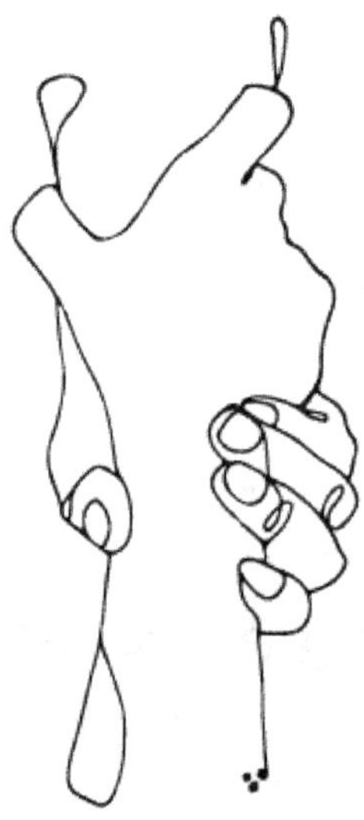

I never thought of myself as weak for staying
with him.

I thought I was strong enough to endure

It wasn't until he was gone that I saw how much
he had taken

My support is **not** to abuse.

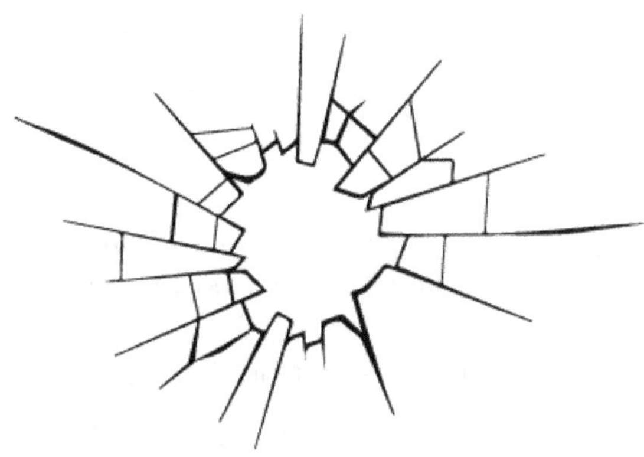

Where am I?

I lost myself in you,
Until I no longer knew who I was

And I've been trying to get back ever since.

If you choose me, you'll *win*.

7

Let me be your **divine move**.

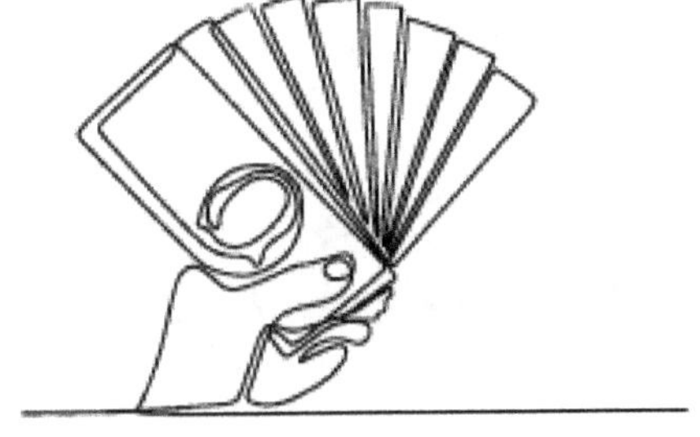

You're the bad investment
I can't stop making.

At least I'm good with money!

How is it possible
That you're my everything

And I'm your nothing?

Crossed wires

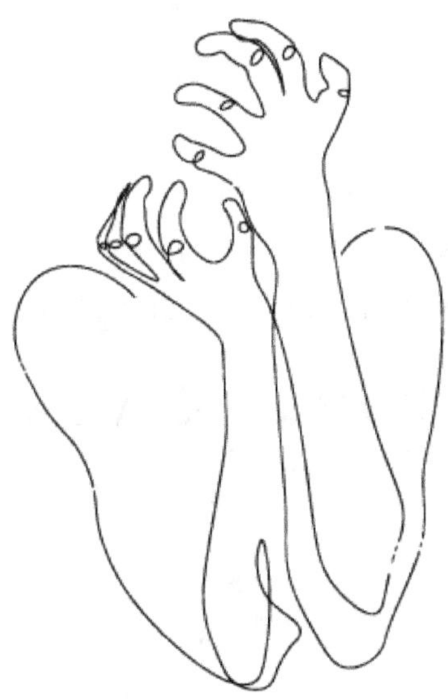

When it rained,
she shone.
Because she felt most comfortable in misery

When did this become my new normal?

It's not crazy to have feelings

You say I'm too sensitive,
But I'm only making up where you lack.

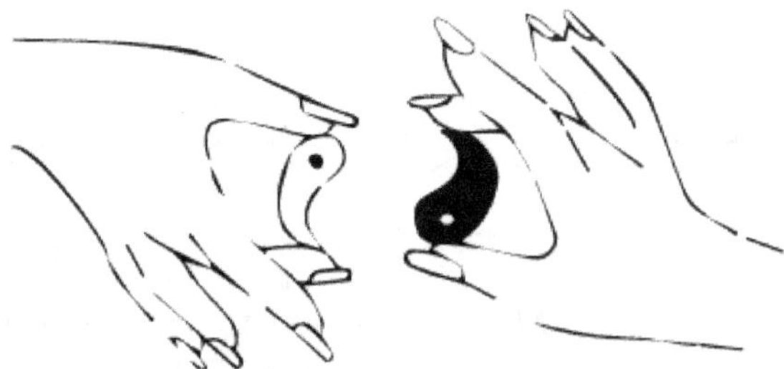

A gift she never should have given.

She taught you how to love yourself
by loving you more than herself.

You make me feel like I'm asking too much,
When I've only ever asked for your love.

It shouldn't be this hard..

Is it on purpose?

Some men wear their scents loud.
Their colognes so intoxicating you can't help but
obsess,
I was always drawn to those men.

But yours is subtle.
Enough so that I find myself drawn in,
Leaning as close as possible to breathe you in.

One word from you would light up my day
So why do you stay away?

That's all it takes.

One word from you would light up my day

There were storms behind her eyes
that made her fierce.

What did she weather?

I'm still trying to find space to shine
in a sky already crowded with stars.

Many bright lights are better than one.

The scars will always be there.
But I'm okay with scars,

It means the wound has finally healed.

Just a few souvenirs.

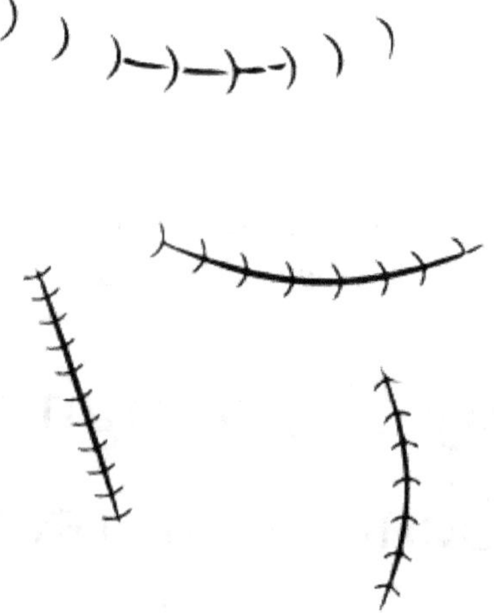

People used to tell me
I brought the **sun** with me,
It took me too long to realize
you brought the *rain*

No wonder I feel so stifled

If it's a choice between chasing him
and keeping your dignity

There are easier marathons to run.

I'm aiming for a 10K

Who is my prince?

I used to wonder what my last love would look
like
Would I ever find my prince?

But now I know, my last love will be my first
The best love I could ask for

My love